PEGGY HORNICK

Qualify To Buy

Expert Tips to Prepare for Homeownership from a Mortgage Pro!

First edition

This book was professionally typeset on Reedsy.
Find out more at reedsy.com

I dedicate this book to all of the homebuyers and clients that have entrusted me with their mortgage needs. It is a true privilege to work in an industry where every day is a chance to make the dream of homeownership a reality. May God's blessings be upon you.

Contents

1

INTRODUCTION

Trying to navigate the homebuying process is often a scary and over-whelming experience!

This could be the biggest financial decision you'll ever make and you'd be surprised how many first timers go into it blindly!

This book was created to take the fear out of the process by providing the reader with the knowledge needed to make wise decisions and not get taken advantage of.

Avoid the landmines and mistakes that could cost you hundreds or even thousands of dollars. Get ready to learn valuable industry lessons from a 40+ year professional who has helped 100's of first time homebuyers achieve their dream of homeownership.

2

AUTHOR'S STORY AND EXPERIENCE

My entry into the mortgage business started rather innocently. In 1981, I was hired through a Temp Agency to wrap Christmas presents for a large mortgage company in California who was known for having extravagant Christmas parties. I must have done a great job wrapping those presents, because they offered me a full time job! I was so naive that when someone asked me to go to the "Doc Department", I went down the hall looking for a Loading Dock!

The most valuable experience I obtained in those early years was floating around all of the departments learning from Loan Processors, Underwriters, Loan Closers and Secondary Marketing. Understanding and getting an overview of the stages in the life of a mortgage was invaluable.

Fast forward to today and I have over 42 years' experience as a successful Mortgage Loan Originator in Florida working directly with borrowers from all walks of life and income brackets. My specialty is helping first time homebuyers have the best homebuying experience possible with no questions left unanswered.

3

BENEFITS OF OWNING A HOME

Homeownership has always been a way to achieve financial stability in America. As of 2023, 66% of Americans own homes with 39% being Baby Boomers and 24% being GenXers. The state with the highest percentage of homeowners is West Virginia at 78% and the state with the lowest percentage of homeowners is New York with only 53%. California comes in second to last with only 55% of residents owning homes.

It's no secret that the super wealthy include real estate as an important part of their wealth portfolio and strategy. Below are some of the main benefits to owning a home:

Financial Benefits:

1. With every monthly mortgage payment you make, you will be building equity in your home. Contrast this to paying rent every month where only the landlord benefits. As home values rise, this is an added bonus to building equity.
2. Your interest rate on a mortgage won't change (if you have a fixed rate) compared to rents that have increased at an alarming rate over the past several years.
3. You can write off your annual mortgage interest as a deduction

on your income taxes. There are other tax deductible items when you bought your home such as loan origination fees and prorated mortgage interest.

4. Other financial benefits may include:

5. If you are self-employed and work from home, you can deduct a portion of your home that you use for your home office.

6. Having on time mortgage payments will increase your credit score which will provide better additional forms of financing as your credit score rises. Ie: Home Equity line of credit, business loan, auto loans.

7. If your new home has room, you can bring in extra income by renting a room or a finished basement via short term rental websites such as AirBnB or by having a longer term tenant. You have the freedom to decide!

Social Benefits:

1. **Generational wealth:** Studies have shown that children of parents that own a home are more likely to be homeowners themselves. This is due to the modeling of homeownership and the security it provides. Real estate is an asset that can be easily transferred to future generations through a trust.

2. **Lower Crime Rates**: Pride in neighborhood and safety of owners are big deterrents for crime compared to highly saturated rental areas. This in turn increases the values of the homes for owners.

3. **Community Participation:** Owners are more likely to remain in their homes for longer periods which brings stability to the neighborhood. "Putting down roots" will encourage more involvement in churches, schools and volunteer organizations which are all needed for a community to thrive.

4

WHAT PRICE HOUSE CAN I AFFORD?

THE IMPORTANCE OF A BUDGET

There are many variables to consider when you have decided to purchase a home. The most important first step is to KNOW your monthly budget… ie…Do you know where every penny of the money coming IN is being spent going OUT? There are many monthly budget templates online but a great free one is Google Spreadsheet for Household Budget. The link is: https://tinyurl.com/bdzrzdff

Take an hour of your time to complete this Household Budget and I guarantee you will be amazed at how much money is flowing out that you can immediately take control of.

As financial expert Dave Ramsey says **"A budget is telling your money where to go instead of wondering where it went."**

A long standing rule of thumb for how much home you can afford is the 28% rule. Your monthly mortgage payment should not cost you more than 28% of your gross income. However, many loan programs allow you to qualify for higher than the 28% rule and with the increased price of homes, higher interest rates and real estate taxes...this is often the case.

By taking an honest accounting of your finances upfront, it will save you the heartache and disappointment of being over-extended in your housing payment. This may mean that you need to lower your expectations for the size and cost of a home you are considering.

HOW MUCH MONEY WILL I NEED FOR A DOWN PAYMENT?

This depends on a few factors. Most first time homebuyers have little money saved for a down payment so they rely on loan programs that provide low down payments.

- **An FHA loan** only requires 3.5% down payment. Ie: A home with a sales price of $300,000 will require a $10,500 down payment. This type of loan requires a credit score above 580 to 600 depending on your lender..
- **A Conventional loan** is typically 5% minimum down payment, however, there are some instances that allow for only 3% down payment. Higher credit scores and median income limits may apply. A Conventional loan requires a 620 credit score.
- **A VA loan** does not require ANY down payment and is offered to anyone who has served in the military. There are length-of-service requirements that will determine the veterans eligibility. 620 is the minimum credit score for VA.
- **A USDA loan** is another loan that does not require any down payment but has maximum income limitations and the property must be in an approved rural or suburban area. A higher score of 640 is required

for USDA loans.

All of the above loans with low down payment requirements are for borrowers that will occupy the home as their primary residence. If you are purchasing a home as your secondary home or as an investment property, you will be required to put more money down.

Also, when your down payment is less than 20%, you will be required to have PMI or Private Mortgage Insurance added to your monthly mortgage payment. This is an "insurance" policy that you pay for, however, it only benefits the lender. VA loans are the exception and do not require PMI.

WAYS TO SAVE FOR THE DOWN PAYMENT

One of my favorite sayings is "It doesn't matter how much you make; it's how much you save". Absolutely everyone can save money...it doesn't have to be a huge amount every month but if you don't start saving now, it will be very difficult to reach your goal of homeownership. Here are some tips on what you can start doing today:

1. **Stop the spending!** If you completed a household budget at the beginning of this chapter, you will quickly realize where the non-essential spending is. If you really want to buy a home, you will have to sacrifice and stop all non-essential buying for a while. You can do without the expensive coffee drinks, going out to dinner, gym membership, movie theaters and unnecessary auto subscriptions. Check your phone settings on how to manage subscriptions that can rack up a lot of money each month.

7

2. **Auto Saving** - Set up an auto deposit directly from your paycheck into a savings account. Most employers will allow you to separate your payroll deposits into two bank accounts. Do not allow transfers from this account to your checking account to avoid the temptation of spending the savings. A rule of thumb is to save 20% of your net earnings per pay period. Although this may be impossible depending on your expenses, any amount will get you moving in the right direction. If you save just $10.00 per day, in one month you will have saved $300 and in a year you will save $3,650!

3. **Sell Stuff** - Do you have furniture, equipment or electronics laying around that haven't been used in awhile? There are many online sights that make selling used items very easy. Just don't forget to put those sales into your savings account!

4. **Sell Your Car?** This next tip is a little harder to hear but so important because it's probably the #1 reason why so many first time homebuyers can't qualify for a mortgage. CAR PAYMENTS! If you really want that home, you may need to sell your car with that big car payment and buy an older car for cash. Your sacrifice today will payoff tomorrow when you have an appreciating asset (home) vs.a depreciating asset (car). Your mortgage professional will calculate your debt ratio and advise if getting rid of that car payment will get you into the home you *want* vs. the home you can *afford*.

5. **Ask for help** - If you are fortunate enough to have a family member with the means to help you with a down payment...by all means ask! Many of my clients get "gifts" from a relative for the down payment and/or closing costs. Just make sure your relative is willing to sign a Gift Letter and provide bank statement information to document where the gift funds came from.

6. **Shared living** - It may be necessary to add a roommate or move back home with a relative for a while to save for a down payment.

This is a quick way to save hundreds of dollars each month for a down payment.

7. **Shop Discount Stores, Sales and Secondhand** - Becoming a thrifty consumer is not only rewarding mentally but it will add dollars to your savings account. Cutting expensive food items out of your diet and grocery cart (soda, bottled water, candy, snacks, name brand laundry soap and hair products, etc) has two benefits...you will save money and become healthier! Trading name brand clothes and luxury items for gently used items or knock offs can save a lot of money! *People won't care what kind of clothes, watch or purse you have when they are still renting and you just bought your new home!*

8. **Pay Cash** - Ease and accessibility of online shopping with free shipping is the number one factor for impulse buying. The average person spends over $300 on impulse purchases every month, according to Slickdeals. If you can change your mindset of needing it NOW to waiting until you can pay cash for an item, you will eliminate impulse buying and save hundreds per month. For most people, this will take a lot of self control but it is worth it if your goal is homeownership.

"We buy things we don't need with money we don't have to impress people we don't like." - Dave Ramsey

HOW TO CALCULATE A MONTHLY MORTGAGE PAYMENT?

The next step to figuring out how much house you can afford is to know the approximate monthly housing expense for the home you are considering. Of course, current interest rates play a big factor in calculating the monthly payment. You can google the current mortgage interest rate by clicking on the following link: http://tinyurl.com/yxr 6a7hj or just type "Today's mortgage rates for 30 Yr. Fixed" in your google search bar. You will need to type in the Loan Amount which is calculated by taking the Sales Price minus the percentage of down payment ($300,000 - 5% = $285,000). Loan amount is $285,000. Next, the dropdown for down payment needs to be selected with the correct amount of down payment. Next, type in your State and credit score range. Choose the interest rate according to the loan type...ie: 30 Yr. Fixed for Conventional; 30 Yr. Fixed FHA for FHA loans and 30 Yr. Fixed VA for VA loans.

Once you have your interest rate, we can go onto the next step.

On the same Google page with the interest rate, scroll down to "Popular Next Steps" and click on "Calculate your Monthly Payment". You can also toggle to "Purchase Budget" to see the approximate income you will need. Fill in the taxes, insurance and HOA dues (if any). This is a great tool to estimate the monthly payments...however, you will still need to speak with a mortgage professional in your area to obtain a formal preapproval.

WHAT IS A DEBT TO INCOME RATIO OR DTI?

Besides your credit score, a debt to income ratio is the single most important calculation in the loan process. It can make or break your chances of getting a loan approval.

So what is a Debt ratio and how is it calculated?

In short, a debt ratio is calculated by dividing all of your monthly debt obligations plus the new housing payment into your gross income. For most loan programs, your debt ratio cannot exceed 50% of your gross income.

For example, your monthly gross income is $5,000. The new housing PITI (principle, interest, taxes and insurance + PMI + HOA dues) is $1,650 and your monthly credit cards and car payment is $650. $1,650 + $650 = $2,300. $2,300 divided by $5,000 = 46% This is an acceptable debt ratio.

What types of debt are included in the debt ratio?

Car payments; installment loan payments; credit card payments using the minimum payment due regardless of how much you pay monthly; student loans - even though they are deferred with no payment due, underwriting guidelines require a payment to be calculated; alimony, child support, IRS tax payment plans.

What is NOT included in the debt ratio?

Monthly rent for the house you are leaving; utility bills, phone bills; car insurance; health insurance.

5

WHY DO I NEED A MORTGAGE PREAPPROVAL?

WHAT IS A MORTGAGE PREQUALIFICATION VS. PREAPPROVAL?

Sometimes, the terms preapproval and prequalification are used interchangeably but they do mean different things.

A **Prequalification** will provide an *estimate* of what you can qualify for without documenting your income, your assets and without pulling your credit.

A **Preapproval** goes more in depth by verifying your income with pay stubs or tax returns; bank statements to confirm funds for the down payment and a credit check.

In most cases, a realtor will require a Preapproval Letter from a Lender in order to show you properties in person and will include the Preapproval Letter with any Contract or Offer. Most Sellers will want to see that you have been preapproved in order to accept your offer..

WHEN SHOULD I GET PREAPPROVED?

I always advise that it's never too early to get preapproved. This is true if you are uncertain about your credit score, job history or income. A mortgage professional can provide you with action items to increase your credit scores, if needed; how much money you need to save for a down payment and what to expect for closing costs.

Once you have your Preapproval Letter, you are ready to start your new home search!

SEEK AN EXPERIENCED MORTGAGE PROFESSIONAL

I cannot stress enough the importance of choosing the right mortgage professional! I take my job and career very seriously due to the sensitive and private information that I obtain from each of my clients. It takes years of experience and knowledge to know how to structure a loan and offer the borrower the best possible loan for their individual scenario. I have rescued many purchases for my clients who started with an inexperienced Loan Officer and were denied a loan due to incorrect or missing information in the loan file that should have been caught at the beginning. These mistakes come with a cost of money, stress and lost time for the borrower. Some of my greatest success stories have been when I can reverse a loan denial by another lender and provide a loan APPROVAL for my clients!

IMPORTANT: If your mortgage professional does not have the patience, time or knowledge to answer your questions, it may be time to choose another professional that comes highly recommended. As a first time homebuyer, you will have lots of questions during the process and you should feel comfortable to call, text or email your Loan Officer with those questions.

It is perfectly acceptable to interview several mortgage loan officers during the selection process. Here are a list of questions you may want to ask:

1. How many years have you been a Loan Officer or worked in the mortgage business?
2. Do you have any upfront charges to do a Preapproval?
3. Can you provide an estimate of your specific Loan fees and interest rate quote?
4. Who will be handling the loan after I complete the application? Where are they located?
5. How long does your loan process take from loan application to closing?
6. Do you have a secure website to upload sensitive documents?

WHAT DOCUMENTS WILL I NEED FOR THE PREAPPROVAL?

Typically, your Loan Officer will want to review the following documents in order to Preapprove you for a mortgage:

W2 Wage Employee:
 – Most recent 30 days of paystubs to calculate base income.

If you are paid overtime, commission or bonus income and need that income to qualify, you may need to provide the last paystub paid in the previous year (ie: pay period ending 12/31/___) so that the fluctuating income can be averaged over a period of time.

-Most recent 2 years of W2 tax forms from all employers during those years.

Self-employed:

-Most recent two years of complete tax returns (all pages) for Individual (1040) and Business Returns (if applicable). Calculating income for self-employed borrowers is more complicated and has many guidelines to adhere to. Loan underwriters use NET income after expenses.

-Most recent 2 years 1099 tax forms for all self employed income

Bank statements - Most recent 2 months of bank statements (all pages) to verify funds for the down payment and closing costs.

Credit report - The Loan Officer will obtain this and advise you of your credit scores.

CREDIT SCORE MYTHS AND FACTS

Most people don't realize that there are several different credit scoring models. These different algorithms serve different purposes. The tri-merge credit reports that we use in the mortgage industry are the most in-depth and cover a longer time period.

A credit report that a credit card company or auto finance company uses is called a Consumer Credit scoring model and typically reports higher scores. If you are monitoring your credit scores from your credit card company or a free online credit score website, your scores could be a lot different than the tri-merge credit scores.

It is important to have your tri-merge credit run as part of the preapproval process. The report will provide 3 scores..Equifax; Experian and TransUnion. Your high and low score will not be used and the middle score will be the score used for the loan qualification.

Impacts on Your Credit Score

- **Payment History** - 35% of your credit scoring is based on your ability to make your payments on time. This is the biggest percentage of weight in scoring. A recent 30 day late can cause a large drop in scores. A foreclosure or bankruptcy have longer and more serious effects on your score.
- **Balances vs. High Credit Limit** - 30% of scoring is based on your credit utilization. A good rule of thumb is to keep your balances at or below 30% of the high credit limit. If you have 5 credit cards and the balances are all close to the high credit limit, your scores will plummet.
- **Length of Credit History** - 15% of scoring will pertain to how long you have established credit. The scoring models like to see at least 12 months of on time payments with established credit before your scores start to increase. The longer your credit history, the higher your scores will be.
- **Credit Variety** - 10% of scoring looks at the different types of credit you have. If you have a mix of credit cards (Revolving) and installment loans (auto loans, student loans, personal loans, mortgages) your scores will benefit.
- **New Credit/Inquiries** - 10% of scoring looks at new debt and inquiries. Your scores could drop by 5 points for 1 inquiry into your credit with a new credit card. Once you start making payments for a few months, your scores will slowly come back up.

MYTH: I don't want to shop for a mortgage lender because they will all pull credit and it will hurt my scores.

FACT: The first hard pull on your credit will drop your scores by only a few points. If you have multiple mortgage companies pulling within the same 2 - 3 week period, it will only count as 1 hit. This allows you to shop for a mortgage lender. A "soft-pull" credit will NOT lower your credit scores. A soft-pull credit is a good option if you are in the early stages of prequalification and shopping for a mortgage lender. Ask your lender if a soft pull credit is available.

MYTH: Opening many credit cards at once won't hurt my credit, especially if it is a promotion.

FACT: Unlike mortgages, revolving credit card inquiries will lower your score each and every time you apply for a card. Don't be tempted by those in-store promotions to open a credit card and get 10% off! Your credit score will suffer!

MYTH: Paying off and/or closing my credit card accounts will improve my scores.

FACT: Your scores may actually DROP if you pay off and close a credit card or installment loan. This is because it may affect your credit mix, your length of credit history or credit utilization ratio.

MYTH: Once I make a payment to lower a balance or pay off a credit card, my scores will increase right away.

FACT: Each creditor reports to the 3 credit repositories at different times during the month. It could take 30-45 days for your credit scores to be affected.

QUICK FIXES TO INCREASE YOUR SCORES BEFORE YOU BUY

1. Check your credit card balances and if possible, pay down the balances to 30% of the high credit limit. If you don't have funds to pay down, ask your creditor to increase the high credit limit which lowers your utilization.

2. Become an Authorized User - If you have a relative or close friend that has a credit card in good standing with low balance to usage ratio and has been opened for at least a year, ask them to add you as an "Authorized User". This will immediately add this good account

to your credit profile. NOTE: If there is a high monthly payment, it may affect your loan qualification and debt ratio.

3. Pay everything on time and bring deferred balances to current.
4. Settle with any Collection accounts on the report. You will need to contact the collection agency and negotiate to settle so they can report the account as paid and settled.
5. Open a Secured Credit Card account with your bank. This type of card requires a cash deposit and you use the issued card to make a purchase and then make on time monthly payments. Ie: You deposit $500.00 and that is your credit limit. You charge $100. and make the minimum $25.00 per month payment. This builds your credit profile.

IS HONESTY THE BEST POLICY?

This will be a short section because the answer is a resounding YES!

I can't tell you how many times issues in a loan file could have been avoided if my client would have been honest and laid all the cards on the table at the time of Preapproval. Let your Mortgage Professional know the good, the bad and the ugly of your financial and income situation upfront so they can better serve you. Don't hide anything because it WILL be discovered by underwriting and background checks that are performed during the loan process.

Mortgage fraud is real and we take it very seriously in our industry. You will sign loan disclosures as part of the closing documents confirming you have not committed loan fraud. Mortgage fraud is investigated by the FBI, so honesty is definitely the BEST policy!

6

WHAT LOAN PROGRAMS ARE RIGHT FOR ME?

4 MOST COMMON LOANS FOR FIRST TIME HOME BUYERS

1. **Conventional** - This is the most common type of loan that is not insured or guaranteed by any federal agency. It can be either *Conforming* (loan limits at or below $750,000 as of the 2024 limit) or *Non-Conforming*, also known as a Jumbo loan, which is any loan over the Conforming loan limit. Typically, it requires a minimum of 5% down payment and in some cases just 3%. If you put less than 20% down, you will be required to have Private Mortgage Insurance (PMI) added to your monthly payment. This loan type is not assumable and has no prepayment penalty. You need a minimum middle credit score of 620 for this loan type. You can get a Conventional loan for a primary, secondary or investment home.

2. **Federal Housing Administration (FHA)** - This Federally insured loan is the most popular program for first time homebuyers because

it only requires a 3.5% down payment and a minimum credit score of 580. You do not need to be a first time homebuyer but you do need to occupy the home as your primary residence. This loan is assumable which makes it attractive to potential buyers when you go to sell as long as your note interest rate is lower than the market rate. You will have monthly Mortgage Insurance regardless of how much down payment you have and it cannot be removed during the life of the FHA loan.

3. **Veterans Administration (VA):** This loan is for Veterans, Servicemembers and surviving spouses and is guaranteed by the VA. No down payment or PMI is required, which makes it a great loan for veterans. Most lenders require a minimum credit score of 620. The interest rate for a VA loan is typically lower than Conventional loans. You will be required to provide a copy of your DD214 Discharge paper to obtain your Certificate of Eligibility.

4. **U.S. Dept. of Agriculture (USDA):** This loan is insured by the US Government and provides loans in approved rural areas with no down payment requirement. However, there are income limits and more strict qualifying guidelines. Most lenders require a credit score of 640 for this type of loan.

PROPERTY TYPES AND HOW IT AFFECTS THE LOAN QUALIFICATION

Not all property types are viewed the same way when it comes to under-writing guidelines or interest rates. This is because some properties are considered more risky or more expensive. A single family home will have a lower interest rate than a condominium, if all other things are equal. If the condo or home in a Planned Unit Development has a monthly HOA, this will affect the amount you can qualify for because the HOA payment must be included in the monthly housing ratio.

A mobile home may require additional down payment as well. Rely on your mortgage professional to provide you with the nuances and requirements for each property type you are considering.

INTEREST RATES, ORIGINATION FEES AND RATE LOCK OPTIONS

I get asked all the time "What are the interest rates going to do in the next couple months?" and my answer is always "If I knew the answer, I'd be a billionaire!"

What I do watch are the trends so that I can provide my clients with advice on what to expect.

Mortgage rates for your loan are directly related to your credit profile. The best interest rates are provided to those with the highest credit scores.

The overall rate environment is driven by many factors such as inflation, the economy, Federal Reserve monetary policy, the Bond Market and the housing market.

To get an idea of what the rates are doing, look at the 10 Yr. Treasury Yield by following this link on Yahoo Finance: https://finance.yahoo.c

om/quote/%5ETNX/ and click the 6 Mo. or Year To Date tab at the top and the graph will show you if rates are trending up or down.

Origination Fees:

Depending on the condition of the interest rate environment, you may have to pay additional Origination Fees or "Discount Point" for the interest rate you choose. The lower the interest rate, the higher the discount points and the higher the interest rate, the lower the discount points. 1 discount point is equal to 1% of your loan amount. Ie: 1.5% discount points for a $200,000 loan amount is $3,000. This charge will be over and above any of the normal closing costs and can significantly increase the cash you need for closing.

Interest Rate Lock Options

There are several times when you can lock in an interest rate during the homebuying process. The best time to lock depends on the immediate interest rate trend. There are some lenders that allow you to Lock and Shop, meaning you can lock an interest rate for 90 days while you are shopping for a home. If the rates drop during the 90 days, you can lower the rate one time. However, this may not be a good idea in a downward rate environment because you will pay more for a 90 day lock vs. a 30 or 15 day lock.

Typically, you will need to lock the interest rate at some point during the loan application process and the length of the lock term will need to be long enough to protect you through the closing date.

The shortest lock length is 15 days and the longest is usually 90 days. The longer the term of the interest rate lock, the higher the cost for the lock.

In an upward trending rate environment, it would be prudent to lock as soon as possible to protect you from the rate increasing during the loan process.

In a downward trending rate environment, you may want to FLOAT with the market and not lock in until 15 days prior to the closing date so that you can take advantage of any rate drops during the loan process.

This may also be a decision that you entrust to your Mortgage Professional since they monitor rates and trends on a daily and sometimes hourly basis.

7

PITFALLS TO AVOID

COMMON MISTAKES DURING PREAPPROVAL AND MORTGAGE PROCESS

These are pretty obvious but during the time between when you've been prequalified, preapproved or applied for your loan:

-DON'T miss a payment or have a late payment on your credit cards, loans or rent

- DON'T switch jobs unless you have discussed with your lender.

- DON'T deposit large amounts of cash into your bank account (all large deposits need

to be sourced and cash is considered non-sourceable)

- DON'T open up any new credit cards

- DON'T close a credit card account (this could drop your credit score)

- DON'T make any large purchases - wait until after the closing date to make sure you have enough funds.

RED FLAGS ON MORTGAGE APPLICATIONS

Mortgage underwriters look for inconsistencies and red flags in the loan application. If you are completing the loan application yourself, it is important to know these red flags:

- Other real estate owned but not disclosed on the application – this includes lots or vacant land.
- Incorrect social security number or more than one social security number for the same person
- Name on application does match name on driver's license
- Current residence address is a PO Box – must list a physical address
- Less than 2 yr. Residence history – must list all addresses in the past 2 years.
- Less than 2 yr. Employment history – must list all jobs in the past 2 years with dates of each job
- Incorrect marital type
- Bank accounts listed that are not in the borrower's name

These are just a few of the red flags. The most important thing to remember is to be completely accurate and truthful when completing a mortgage loan application.

8

DO I NEED A REALTOR?

With so many websites listing homes for sale within minutes of them going on the market, you may be tempted to 'go it alone' when buying a home. While there are some success stories, I hear many more "I wish I would have worked with a realtor" stories. Realtors provide a valuable service to buyers at no cost so you have nothing to lose!

THE ROLE OF A REALTOR FOR A BUYER

It is the duty of the realtor to make sure you are preapproved for a mortgage, know the price range and loan type you are preapproved for and search for homes in your price range. A realtor will have access to MLS listings that you cannot access and they will schedule showings with the listing agents.

BENEFITS OF USING A REALTOR

- A realtor will save you hours of time searching for a home since they do all the research and neighborhood analysis to find the home that meets your criteria.
- An experienced realtor will have connections with other realtors to search for "pocket listings" or homes that are "coming soon" that have not been entered into the MLS system yet.
- If you are relocating to a new area, the local realtor will know the neighborhoods, schools, churches and businesses in that area better than any website.
- A realtor doesn't get paid until they find you a home which means they will work harder for you than you realize. Their compensation comes from the Seller of the listed property so you are not the one paying them for their services but their fiduciary responsibility is to you. A win for buyers.
- Unlike most industries, a seasoned realtor is paid the same as a new realtor. Choose wisely!
- A Realtor is your advocate if things don't go as planned. They can seek legal counsel, consult with the listing agent, negotiate on your behalf and do everything they can to keep the transaction moving forward.

9

MY OFFER WAS ACCEPTED, NOW WHAT?

MORTGAGE MILESTONES AND TIMELINE

In the first couple of weeks after your offer has been accepted, there will be a flurry of activity and appointments. You will be receiving emails and calls from your realtor, your mortgage lender, the title company and home inspector who are all working with time deadlines. Time is the essence to respond to each request! Below are some of the main milestones:

1. You may be required to provide a **Good Faith or Escrow Deposit** as part of the contract to show the Seller you are serious about your offer to buy their property. If so, you will have a short period of time (usually a few days) to provide this money to the realtor to be held in "escrow" for the duration of the process. This amount will be credited at closing towards your down payment and closing costs.

2. **Loan Application with supporting documents** – You will need to complete the loan application along with state required disclosures

within the first 3 business days from the date of the contract. You will need to provide your income documents, bank statements and any other items your mortgage professional has requested in order to submit your loan to underwriting for a formal approval.

3. **Home Inspection** - If you are having a home inspection done, you will have a short period of time to complete this per the purchase contract. You will need to schedule with an inspector of your choice as soon as possible.

4. **Appraisal** - Your lender will order the appraisal from an appraisal management company who assigns an independent and non-biased appraiser. This is a big milestone in the loan process because it provides the market value of the home you are buying based on other sales in the neighborhood within the past 6 months. If the value is lower than the sales price, your loan may be denied due to the minimum loan-to-value not being met.

Below are a few negotiation options that can take place to overcome this issue:

a. Ask the Seller to reduce the sales price to match the appraised value.

b. Provide a larger down payment to meet the loan-to-value requirement. This can also be a combination of the seller reducing the sales price and the buyer making a larger down payment.

c. Withdraw from buying the home and cancel the contract. If the value is significantly lower, it is a sign that the home is overpriced for the neighborhood and may be a poor investment.

5. **Underwriting Approval** - The lender will receive a Loan Approval from the underwriter which means that all the documentation you have provided has been reviewed and verified. The lender may ask you for additional information or "conditions" that need to be met before the loan can be finalized.

6. **Clear To Close!** - These are my 3 favorite words! All underwriting

conditions have been met and it is time to schedule the closing date and time.

7. **Closing Day** - Congratulations on all of the hard work you have done to become a homeowner! This day may be the best day ever but it can also be a little overwhelming. You will need to wire funds to the title agent or closing attorney; you may also have a final walk through of the home to make sure the seller has left it in the same condition when you initially previewed the home; you will sign the final Closing Documents package which transfers ownership and title to you and you may have movers to coordinate!

As for the mortgage and closing costs, there should be no surprises or changes on the final closing documents. By law, you will have received from your mortgage lender the initial Closing Disclosure three business days prior to the closing date. Make sure you review and address any questions you have BEFORE you get to the closing table.

10

CONCLUSION

It has been a labor of love and an outpouring of my 42 years of mortgage experience and knowledge to write this book. My goal is to make your home buying experience a little easier and smoother with the information in this book.

Did you find this resource helpful? I would be forever grateful if you could leave a review on Amazon for this book. This will help others find this book in the search engine so they can benefit just as you have.

I wish you many happy years in your new home!

11

GLOSSARY OF MORTGAGE TERMS

1. **Amortization:** The process of paying off a mortgage loan through regular payments, where each installment includes both principal and interest.
2. **Annual Percentage Rate (APR):** The total cost of a mortgage stated as a yearly rate, including interest, points, and other fees.
3. **Appraisal:** A professional assessment of the value of a property, conducted by a licensed appraiser.
4. **Closing Costs:** The fees and charges associated with the purchase of a home, including loan origination fees, title insurance, and attorney fees.
5. **Collateral:** Property used to secure a loan. In the case of a mortgage, the home being financed is the collateral.
6. **Credit Score:** A numerical representation of a borrower's creditworthiness, based on credit history and other financial behavior.
7. **Down Payment:** The initial payment made by the buyer, usually a percentage of the home's purchase price, paid upfront.
8. **Equity:** The value of a homeowner's interest in their property, calculated as the property's current market value minus any out-

standing mortgage debt.

9. **Fixed-Rate Mortgage:** A mortgage with a constant interest rate that does not change over the life of the loan.

10. **Foreclosure:** The legal process by which a lender reclaims a property when the borrower fails to make mortgage payments.

11. **Homeowners Association (HOA):** An organization that manages common areas and amenities in a planned community, usually financed by homeowner fees.

12. **Interest Rate:** The percentage of the loan amount charged by the lender for borrowing the money.

13. **Loan-to-Value Ratio (LTV):** The ratio of the loan amount to the appraised value of the property, expressed as a percentage.

14. **Mortgage Broker:** A professional who connects borrowers with lenders and helps them find a suitable mortgage.

15. **Origination Fee:** A fee charged by lenders for processing a loan application.

16. **PITI:** An acronym representing the four components of a mortgage payment: Principal, Interest, Taxes, and Insurance.

17. **Pre-Approval:** A process in which a lender reviews a borrower's financial information and provides a preliminary commitment for a loan amount.

18. **Private Mortgage Insurance (PMI):** Insurance that protects the lender in case the borrower defaults on the loan, typically required for loans with a down payment less than 20%.

19. **Refinancing:** The process of replacing an existing mortgage with a new one, often to obtain a lower interest rate or change the loan terms.

20. **Title Insurance:** Insurance that protects the homeowner and lender against any disputes over the ownership of the property.

21. **Underwriting:** The process by which a lender evaluates a borrower's creditworthiness and the risk associated with granting

a mortgage loan.

12

RESOURCES

Taylor, M. (2023, July 25). *Homeowner data and statistics 2023*. Bankrate. https://www.bankrate.com/homeownership/home-ownership-statistics/#:~:text=and%20future%20homeowners.-,Key%20homeowner%20data%202023,decade%20between%201950%20and%202010.
https://www.bankrate.com/homeownership/home-ownership-statistics/#:~:text=and%20future%20homeowners.-,Key%20homeowner%20data%202023,decade%20between%201950%20and%202010.

Esajian, J., & Esajian, J. (2022, December 7). *15 Benefits Of Homeownership You May Have Never Considered*. FortuneBuilders. https://www.fortunebuilders.com/benefits-of-homeownership/
https://www.fortunebuilders.com/benefits-of-homeownership/

Fuscaldo, D. (2022, June 14). *How to set a budget for buying your first home*. Investopedia. https://www.investopedia.com/personal-finance/how-set-budget-your-first-home/#:~:text=A%20good%20rule%20of%20thumb,your%20gross%20earnings%20each%20month.
https://www.investopedia.com/personal-finance/how-set-budget-your-first-home/#:~:text=A%20good%20rule%20of%20thumb,your

%20gross%20earnings%20each%20month.

HOUSEHOLD BUDGET TEMPLATE_Google-Sheet. (n.d.). Google Docs. https://docs.google.com/spreadsheets/d/189R_NT16DIlh1QwyUymVqF m2nwSe4Yxa0h71yjy5UFI/edit#gid=0
   https://docs.google.com/spreadsheets/d/189R_NT16DIlh1QwyUym VqFm2nwSe4Yxa0h71yjy5UFI/edit#gid=0

Brophy, M., & Rivera, D. (2023, July 26). 16 Impulse buying statistics Retailers should know in 2023. *Fit Small Business.* https://fitsmallbusine ss.com/impulse-buying-statistics/
   https://fitsmallbusiness.com/impulse-buying-statistics/

Akin, J. (2023, July 29). *What affects your credit scores?* https://www.expe rian.com/blogs/ask-experian/credit-education/score-basics/what-aff ects-your-credit-scores/
   https://www.experian.com/blogs/ask-experian/credit-education/sc ore-basics/what-affects-your-credit-scores/

Barroso, A., & O'Shea, B. (2023, November 7). *How to improve credit Fast.* NerdWallet. https://www.nerdwallet.com/article/finance/raise-credit-score-fast
   https://www.nerdwallet.com/article/finance/raise-credit-score-fas t

Maverick, J. (2021, August 12). *The most important factors affecting mortgage rates.* Investopedia. https://www.investopedia.com/mortg age/mortgage-rates/factors-affect-mortgage-rates/
   https://www.investopedia.com/mortgage/mortgage-rates/factors-affect-mortgage-rates/

What are common red flags that may indicate mortgage fraud? (n.d.).
https://selling-guide.fanniemae.com/Selling-Guide/Doing-Busines
s-with-Fannie-Mae/Subpart-A3-Getting-Started-with-Fannie-Mae/
Chapter-A3-4-Lending-Practices/1074102041/What-are-common-re
d-flags-that-may-indicate-mortgage-fraud.htm

https://selling-guide.fanniemae.com/Selling-Guide/Doing-Busine
ss-with-Fannie-Mae/Subpart-A3-Getting-Started-with-Fannie-Ma
e/Chapter-A3-4-Lending-Practices/1074102041/What-are-common-
red-flags-that-may-indicate-mortgage-fraud.htm

About the Author

Peggy Hornick is a seasoned professional with a successful 42 yr. career in the mortgage industry. She is a dedicated advocate for aspiring homeowners and her experience and knowledge has been the driving force behind her success.

As an author, Peggy goes beyond the technicalities of mortgages, infusing the book with a personal touch that stems from a genuine passion for helping people achieve their home ownership goals. Whether you're a first-time home buyer or looking to refine your approach to mortgage qualification, Peggy provides invaluable insights and expert tips to pave the way to successful home ownership.

Peggy is a Mortgage Loan Originator and business owner in the beautiful state of Florida. She continues to help her clients with their mortgage needs and provides educational seminars and support to realtor organizations.

She has been married for 26 years with 3 adult children and 3 beautiful

Grandsons!

If you would like to contact Peggy Hornick, please email her at peggy@ecmortgagelenders.com